WORLD HERITAGE

Protecting the Human Story

Brendan and Debbie Gallagher

This edition first published in 2011 in the United States of America by Smart Apple Media. All rights reserved. No part of this book may be reproduced in any form or by any means without written permission from the publisher.

Smart Apple Media
P.O. Box 3263
Mankato, MN, 56002

First published in 2010 by
MACMILLAN EDUCATION AUSTRALIA PTY LTD
15–19 Claremont St, South Yarra, Australia 3141

Visit our web site at www.macmillan.com.au or go directly to www.macmillanlibrary.com.au

Associated companies and representatives throughout the world.

Copyright © Brendan and Debbie Gallagher 2010

Library of Congress Cataloging-in-Publication Data

Gallagher, Brendan.
   Protecting the human story / Brendan and Debbie Gallagher.
      p. cm. — (World heritage.)
   Includes index.
   ISBN 978-1-59920-581-6 (library bound)
   1. Historic sites—Conservation and restoration—Juvenile literature. 2. Cultural property—Protection—Juvenile literature.
   3. World Heritage areas—Juvenile literature. I. Gallagher, Debbie, 1969– II. Title.
   CC135.G35 2011
   363.6'9—dc22
                           2009053018

Publisher: Carmel Heron
Managing Editor: Vanessa Lanaway
Editor: Kirstie Innes-Will
Proofreader: Paige Amor
Designer: Kerri Wilson
Page layout: Kerri Wilson
Photo researcher: Legend Images
Illustrator: Guy Holt
Production Controller: Vanessa Johnson

Manufactured in China by Macmillan Production (Asia) Ltd.
Kwun Tong, Kowloon, Hong Kong
Supplier Code: CP December 2009

Acknowledgments
The author and the publisher are grateful to the following for permission to reproduce copyright material:

Cover photograph of wooden sculptures at Osun Grove, Osogbo, Nigeria courtesy of Picture Media/Reuters/George Esiri

Photographs courtesy of:
AAP Image/Grenville Turner/Wildlight, 31; © Auschwitz-Birkenau State-Museum. Photo: Paweł Sawicki, 8, 9; © Yann Arthus-Bertrand/Corbis, 6; © John Carnemolla/Corbis, 30; © Roger de la Harpe/Corbis, 19; © Chris Hellier/Corbis, 7; Lucy Roberts, Department of Conservation, New Zealand, 29; Pierre-Olivier Fortin, 13; Frans Lemmens/Getty Images, 24; Hideaki Tanaka/Sebun Photo/Getty Images, 20; © Konrad Kaminski/iStockphoto, 10; © Mary Lane/iStockphoto, 12; Photolibrary © AAD Worldwide Travel Images/Alamy, 21; Photolibrary/Sylvain Grandadam, 18; Photolibrary/Knut Schulz, 25; Picture Media/Reuters/George Esiri, 1, 22, 23; © Sam Dcruz/Shutterstock, 11; © Christopher Elwell/Shutterstock, 17; © Curtis Kautzer/Shutterstock, 26; © Graeme Knox/Shutterstock, 28; © Alex Neauville/Shutterstock, 14; © SVLumagraphica/Shutterstock, 27; USA Library of Congress, 15; Wikimedia Commons photo by Jason Smith, 16.

While every care has been taken to trace and acknowledge copyright, the publisher tenders their apologies for any accidental infringement where copyright has proved untraceable. Where the attempt has been unsuccessful, the publisher welcomes information that would redress the situation.

Please note
At the time of printing, the Internet addresses appearing in this book were correct. Owing to the dynamic nature of the Internet, however, we cannot guarantee that all these addresses will remain correct.

Contents

When a word in the text is printed in **bold**, look for its meaning in the glossary boxes.

World Heritage

There are places around the world that are important to all peoples. We call these places the world's heritage. Some of these places are human creations, such as the pyramids of Egypt. Some are natural creations, such as the Great Barrier Reef of Australia.

The World Heritage List

The World Heritage List is a list of **sites** that must be protected because they have some kind of outstanding importance for the world. This list was created in 1972, and new places are added every year. Each site on the World Heritage List belongs to one of the following categories:

 NATURAL – for example, waterfalls, forests, or deserts

 CULTURAL – for example, a building or a site where an event occurred

 MIXED – if it has both natural and cultural features

UNESCO

UNESCO, the United Nations Educational, Scientific, and Cultural Organization, is the organization that maintains the World Heritage List. Find out more at www.unesco.org.

World Heritage Criteria

A place can be **inscribed** on the World Heritage List if it meets at least one of these ten **criteria** and is an outstanding example of it. The criteria are:

 i a masterpiece of human creative genius

 ii a site representing the sharing of human ideas

 iii a site representing a special culture or civilization

 iv a historical building or landscape from a period of history

 v a site representing or important to a traditional culture

 vi a site representing an important event, idea, living tradition, or belief

 vii a very beautiful or unique natural site

 viii a site showing evidence of Earth's history

 ix an important ecosystem

 x an important natural habitat for species protection

KEY TERMS

sites	places
inscribed	added to
criteria	rules or requirements

4

Protecting the Human Story

Protecting the Human Story is about protecting great human ideas. The "human story" is the story of all peoples around the world – their cultures, their beliefs, and how they developed. It is about big ideas and events that changed history, and the places associated with them. It also includes **living traditions** in the places where traditional societies still live today. Their land and its features remind them of great events in the past or are important for their beliefs.

 ## Criteria for Protecting the Human Story

Many of the places in this book are important for several reasons. This book focuses on one main reason: how a place is linked to an important event, idea, living tradition, or belief. This is reason vi on the list of criteria for being on the World Heritage List. This book also includes some sites important for reason iii, sites representing a special culture or **civilization**.

Protecting World Heritage

Governments around the world have all agreed to protect the sites on the World Heritage List. A site that is not being properly looked after may be put on the List of World Heritage in Danger. See http://whc.unesco.org/en/158/

This map shows the location of the World Heritage sites covered in this book.

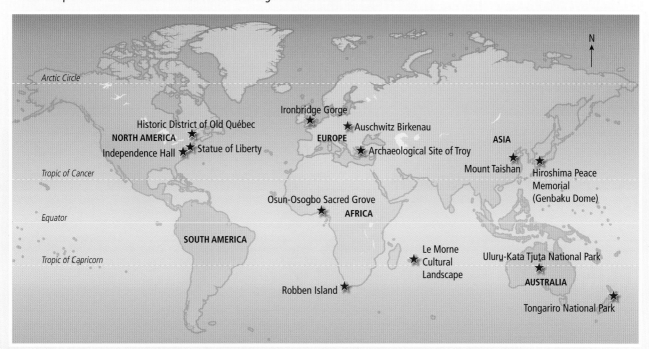

living traditions   traditions that continue to be practiced in a culture today

civilization   the culture and society of a particular group in history

Archaeological Site of Troy

Archaeological Site of Troy is the ruins of an ancient **citadel** on the west coast of Turkey. In the 1200s B.C., the city was at the center of the Trojan War. This war was fought between Mycenae and Troy over trading and money.

Troy is one of the most famous archaeological sites in the world and is considered by many to be the birthplace of archaeology.

FACT FILE

★ TURKEY

Troy protects the ideas of the great writer Homer, who wrote a famous poem about it.

Category: ✋

Criteria: 🔁 🔺 🌐

plains below hill

Great Hall

citadel of Troy

TIMELINE

4th millennium B.C.	1300 B.C.	730 B.C.	A.D 1870	1998
People begin to settle in the Troy area.	The Trojan War is probably fought around this time.	The poet Homer recites his version of the Trojan War to public audiences.	Heinrich Schliemann begins digging into the ruins at Troy.	The site is inscribed on the World Heritage List.

Important Features

The Trojan War played a central role in one of the greatest works of ancient writing, *The Illiad*, by the poet Homer. Illion is another name for Troy. *The Illiad* tells the story, in a poetic style, of the humans and the gods thought to have taken part in the Trojan War. Homer's work has inspired writers, sculptors, composers, and painters for thousands of years.

This relief is of Priam, the king of Troy, begging for the body of Hector, his son, to be returned by the warrior Achilles.

Issues

The walls at Troy are very delicate, so **conservationists** have made mud-brick walls to support weak sections. The have also made sure that there is a system to drain water away from the ruins. The site receives around 250,000 visitors a year, so a visitor center is being built to organize their movement and to house many of the ancient objects found by **archaeologists**.

GLOSSARY

archaeological	to do with studying cultures from their remains
citadel	fortress in or near a city
conservationists	people who protect an area
archaeologists	people who study civilizations from their remains

Auschwitz Birkenau

Auschwitz Birkenau, Poland, was a German Nazi **extermination** camp that operated during World War II. Today, Auschwitz Birkenau is a symbol of hope, because it reminds us of the strength of the human spirit and the human ability to overcome even the most terrible events.

FACT FILE

POLAND

Auschwitz Birkenau protects evidence of the Holocaust, the mass murder of Jews in World War II.

Category: ✋

Criteria: 🤲

Auschwitz is the site of one of the worst crimes ever committed.

prisoner barracks

electric fences with barbed wire

guard tower

TIMELINE

1939	1940	1942	1942–44	1944	1979
Nazi Germany invades Poland, starting World War II in Europe.	Auschwitz Birkenau is built and thousands of Polish Jews are imprisoned there.	Gas extermination chambers are built at Auschwitz Birkenau.	Tens of thousands of Jews and other peoples are transported to Auschwitz Birkenau where they are killed.	The Nazis try to destroy Auschwitz as the Russian army advances.	Auschwitz Birkenau is inscribed on the World Heritage List.

At the Auschwitz Birkenau camp 1.1 million people, mostly Jews, were killed.

Important Features

Auschwitz Birkenau was the main and largest Nazi extermination camp. Buildings at Auschwitz Birkenau, with its barbed wire fences, gas chambers, and **cremation** area, are kept in the condition they were in after World War II. These buildings remind us of the terrible events that occurred there.

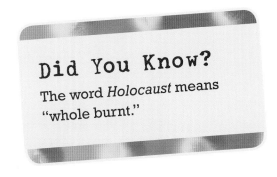

Did You Know?
The word *Holocaust* means "whole burnt."

Issues

There was concern that plans for a nearby road would impact on the landscape around Auschwitz Birkenau. Not only would the road have had a visual impact on the site, but noise from the road would have been heard in the area. The quietness of Auschwitz Birkenau is considered an essential feature of the area. Authorities are now planning an alternative route for the road.

GLOSSARY

extermination   killing or destroying
cremation   the act of burning bodies

Hiroshima Peace Memorial (Genbaku Dome)

Hiroshima Peace Memorial (Genbaku Dome) is the only building that remained standing after an **atomic bomb** was dropped on the city of Hiroshima, Japan, in 1945. Genbaku Dome is maintained as a symbol of hope for world peace and the elimination of all **nuclear weapons**.

FACT FILE

JAPAN

The Hiroshima Peace Memorial protects evidence of the first time a nuclear weapon was used on humans.

Category: ✋

Criteria: 🌐

Many Japanese people view the dome as a symbol of the destructive power of nuclear weapons.

metal dome frame

shattered walls

no interior rooms

TIMELINE

1915	1937	1941	1945	1966	1996
The Hiroshima Commercial Exhibition Hall is built.	Japan invades China, starting the Second Sino-Japanese War.	Japan bombs Pearl Harbor, making the Second Sino-Japanese War part of World War II.	On August 6, the United States drops a nuclear bomb on Hiroshima.	The Genbaku Dome is renamed Hiroshima Peace Memorial.	The site is inscribed on the World Heritage List.

Important Features

The Hiroshima Peace Memorial, a five-storey building with a copper dome on top, was about 2,034 feet (620 meters) from the center of the atomic bomb's blast. The building was shattered, with some rooms and walls destroyed. However, because the blast came almost directly from above, the core of the building remained standing.

Issues

The skeleton and metal dome of the Genbaku Dome are intact. However, the building is very delicate. Experts have used special glues to stop the dome from collapsing. **Conservationists** are careful to make sure the outside of the building looks almost exactly like it did after the atomic bomb blast.

Did You Know?

Hundreds of thousands of people were affected by the explosion at Hiroshima, and 140,000 people died.

Metal reinforcements prop up the interior walls of the Hiroshima Peace Memorial.

GLOSSARY

atomic bomb	bomb powered from the process of splitting atoms
nuclear weapons	very powerful weapons that use atomic energy
conservationists	people who protect an area

Historic District of Old Québec

The Historic District of Old Québec in Canada was built as a French **colony** in the 1600s. Almost half of the buildings in the Historic District were built before 1850. The city's buildings and **fortifications** are associated with the settlement of Europeans in North America.

FACT FILE

CANADA

The Historic District of Old Québec protects evidence of the **colonial** period in the history of North America.

Category:

Criteria:

Samuel de Champlain chose the site for Québec because it was a natural harbor for ships and high enough to watch for danger.

Chateau Frontenac

city walls (fortifications)

old houses

Saint Lawrence River

TIMELINE

1608	1663	1759	1763	1870s	1985
Québec City is founded by French explorer Samuel de Champlain.	Québec becomes the capital of New France.	British forces capture Québec City.	Britain takes over most French territories in the Americas.	The city decides to preserve the city walls and fortifications.	The site is inscribed on the World Heritage List.

Important Features

At first, the colony of Québec grew only slowly, but after it became the capital of New France churches, hospitals, and many houses were built. French engineers also built walls and other fortifications to protect the city from attack by British war ships. Chateau Frontenac is the largest building in Old Québec.

Issues

In 2008, one of Québec's colonial buildings, the Drill Hall, burned down. There are plans to restore the building using plans and photographs of the original building. The entire inside of the Drill Hall will be rebuilt according to its original design.

Only the outside of the Drill Hall remained after the fire in 2008.

GLOSSARY

colony	a group of people who settle in a new country but keep a connection to their home country
fortifications	things built to strengthen or protect an area
colonial	to do with colonies

Independence Hall

Independence Hall is a red brick building in the city of Philadelphia. In 1776, one of the most important events in American history took place here – the signing of the **Declaration of Independence**.

FACT FILE

UNITED STATES

Independence Hall protects the site where important documents to do with freedom and democracy were signed.

Category:

Criteria:

Independence Hall is an important landmark in the development of freedom and democracy in the United States.

bell tower

red brick building

room where Declaration was signed

TIMELINE

A.D. 1732–53	1776	1787	1979
The Independence Hall is built.	The Declaration of Independence is signed at Independence Hall.	The Constitution of the United States is signed at Independence Hall.	Independence Hall is inscribed on the World Heritage List.

Important Features

The Declaration of Independence contains words that are important to all peoples. It states that "all men are created equal" and that all have a right to "Life, Liberty, and the pursuit of Happiness." Another important document, the **Constitution** of the United States, was also signed at Independence Hall. It guarantees freedom and equality for the peoples of the United States. Many countries have been inspired to include the same principles in their own constitutions.

Issues

The original documents of the Declaration and the Constitution used to be housed in sealed glass cases filled with gas. However, the glass began to deteriorate, so the documents were removed from the cases in 2001. Dirt, grime, and glue, used in the past to protect them, were cleaned from the documents. Worn edges were repaired to prevent them becoming worse. The Declaration and Constitution have now been placed in new cases to protect them.

Did You Know?

The Declaration of Independence was signed during the American Revolution, a war between the United States and Britain that lasted from 1775 to 1783.

This is the original document of the Declaration of Independence.

GLOSSARY

Declaration of Independence the document declaring independence for the peoples of the United States from Great Britain

constitution a document that lays out the principles on which a country will be run

Ironbridge Gorge

Ironbridge Gorge in the United Kingdom is a **gorge** that is full of mines and workshops dating from the 1700s. An important event in human history called the **Industrial Revolution** began here and spread from this area to countries around the world.

FACT FILE

UNITED KINGDOM

Ironbridge Gorge protects the place where the Industrial Revolution began.

Category:

Criteria:

Ironbridge was the first metal bridge ever built.

Ironbridge

gorge

River Severn

TIMELINE

1709	1779–81	1700s–1800s	1986
In Ironbridge Gorge, Abraham Darby I uses coal to produce iron.	Abraham Darby III builds Ironbridge.	The area becomes an inspiration to writers and artists.	Ironbridge Gorge is inscribed on the World Heritage List.

Every few years, the River Severn breaks its banks, flooding the valley and causing damage to the World Heritage site.

Important Features

In 1709, Abraham Darby I invented a new way of using coal to make iron using a **blast furnace**. It meant iron could be produced in huge amounts cheaply. Without his discovery, the Industrial Revolution could not have taken place. His grandson, Abraham Darby III, built the bridge called Ironbridge, the first large structure made from **cast iron**. It led to the creation of other cast iron structures, including the Sydney Harbour Bridge in Australia and Brooklyn Bridge in the United States.

Issues

The bridge at Ironbridge has been damaged by flooding several times. Protection barriers are being put in place to stop the River Severn from affecting the bridge.

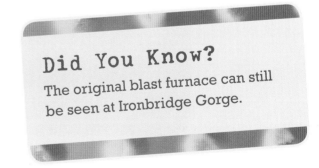

Did You Know?
The original blast furnace can still be seen at Ironbridge Gorge.

GLOSSARY

gorge	narrow, steep-sided valley
Industrial Revolution	change in a society from farming to industry
blast furnace	oven used to make iron
cast iron	strong iron that can be molded into different shapes

Le Morne Cultural Landscape

Le Morne Cultural Landscape is centered around an **extinct** volcano on the island of Mauritius. During the 1700s and early 1800s, Mauritius was an important port for transporting slaves between Asia, Africa, and the Americas. Le Morne is a powerful symbol of the fight for freedom from slavery.

FACT FILE

AFRICA
MAURITIUS

Le Morne protects the place where many slaves escaped by hiding on or around Le Morne Mountain.

Category:

Criteria:

extinct volcano

steep cliffs

Indian Ocean

thick vegetation

The extinct volcano of Le Morne has very steep cliffs and thick vegetation. This made it an ideal place for escaped slaves to hide.

TIMELINE

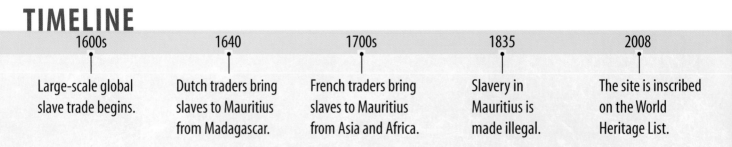

1600s	1640	1700s	1835	2008
Large-scale global slave trade begins.	Dutch traders bring slaves to Mauritius from Madagascar.	French traders bring slaves to Mauritius from Asia and Africa.	Slavery in Mauritius is made illegal.	The site is inscribed on the World Heritage List.

Many of the people of Mauritius are descended from maroons.

Important Features

Around 1820, more than one tenth of slaves on Mauritius, called *maroons*, escaped. Some tried to flee by boat. Others hid on the steep slopes of Le Morne Mountain – they risked their lives by climbing the cliffs. The **oral history** of Mauritius says that many maroons leapt off Le Morne to their deaths rather than be recaptured.

Issues

Plans to build hotels and other buildings near the mountain are the biggest threat to Le Morne. For the people of Mauritius, Le Morne is a **sacred** place. It is important to **preserve** Le Morne as it was when it was a place of hope and freedom for hundreds of maroons.

Did You Know?

At least 330,000 people were transported as slaves to Mauritius and its sister island, Réunion, between 1670 and 1835.

GLOSSARY

extinct	dead, no longer active
oral history	the story of the past told in spoken words or song
sacred	holy, religious
preserve	to protect or keep safe

Mount Taishan

Mount Taishan, in northeast China, is one of the most important **sacred** places for the Chinese peoples. It is important for many different reasons. For instance, it is associated with the development of writing and with the great **philosopher** Confucius, who climbed the mountain around 500 B.C..

FACT FILE

CHINA

Taishan protects one of the birthplaces of Chinese civilization and where the Chinese **empire** was first declared.

Category:

Criteria:

Jade Emperor Peak

temple

steps

The stone stairway up Mount Taishan is 5.6 miles (9 kilometers) in length.

TIMELINE

5000 B.C.	Around 500 B.C.	219 B.C.	A.D. 1987
Taishan begins to be worshipped by local people.	Confucius climbs Taishan.	Qin Shi Huang, the first Chinese **emperor**, declares the unity of his empire on Taishan.	Taishan is inscribed on the World Heritage List.

Important Features

Taishan is a combination of forest and built features blending in harmony with one another. The 22 temples on the mountain are devoted to different religions. The mountain is seen as the first and greatest of China's five sacred mountains. Over 3,000 years, 72 emperors came to Taishan to make sacrifices and carry out special ceremonies. The mountain is also a source of inspiration for Chinese artists, scholars, and philosophers.

Did You Know?

There are 6,600 steps in the climb to the peak of Mount Taishan.

There are 1,018 stone and cliffside inscriptions on Taishan.

Issues

In 1998, there was concern about the impact of humans on Taishan. More than 2 million people visit it each year. A lot of people were selling souvenirs and food in stalls on the mountain, placing advertising boards along the paths or building houses wherever they could. This was destroying the character of the mountain. By 2003 the Taishan managers had removed a lot of the advertising boards, garbage, and illegal stalls and houses. They also discovered 200 sacred trees and stone inscriptions that had been concealed in the courtyards of the houses.

GLOSSARY

sacred	holy, religious
philosopher	a thinker
empire	a group of nations and kingdoms with one ruler
emperor	ruler of an empire

Osun-Osogbo Sacred Grove

Osun-Osogbo Sacred Grove is a **grove** of **shrines**, artistic works, and sculptures, located within a **rain forest** near the city of Osogbo, in Nigeria. The grove is central to the culture of the Yoruba people, who have lived in this part of Africa for thousands of years.

FACT FILE

The Osun-Osogbo Sacred Grove protects a symbol of the identity of the Yoruba people.

Category:

Criteria:

Many of the artistic works and shrines in the grove are dedicated to Osun, a goddess of love, beauty, and wealth.

dense rain forest

shrine

wooden sculpture

TIMELINE

Early 1600s	1965	2005
The Yoruba people establish the city of Osogbo.	The grove is declared a national monument of Nigeria.	The site is inscribed on the World Heritage List.

Important Features

Groves were once common outside Yoruba towns, but Osun-Osogbo Sacred Grove is the last such grove in western Africa. It contains five **sacred** spaces and 40 shrines. The Osun river that cuts through the grove is named after the goddess Osun, who the Yoruba believe lives in the grove. The Yoruba people hold a festival at the grove once a year, renewing the bonds between the people, the ruler of Osogbo, and the goddess.

Issues

The grove is located in an ancient rain forest. Thirty percent of the rain forest has been converted into plantations and other uses. There are plans to replant and regrow the rain forest in these areas.

Asa dancers perform a ritual dance in the Yoruba festival at Osogbo.

GLOSSARY

grove	a garden or small area of trees
shrines	places for worship
rain forest	forest that gets a lot of rain
sacred	holy, religious

Robben Island

Robben Island is a small South African island that was used as a prison for over 300 years. In 1962, the island was used to imprison those who opposed **apartheid**. Apartheid meant that non-white people were only allowed to live in certain areas and do certain types of work.

Robben Island is a symbol of freedom and the triumph of the human spirit over terrible difficulties.

South Africa

Cape Town

Robben Island

TIMELINE

1498	1658	1962	1990	1991	1994	1999
European explorers reach Robben Island.	The first prisoner is held on Robben Island.	South Africa begins using Robben Island as a prison for those protesting apartheid.	Nelson Mandela is released, after being imprisoned since 1964.	The last political prisoners leave Robben Island.	Nelson Mandela becomes president of South Africa.	Robben Island is inscribed on the World Heritage List.

Nelson Mandela was the most famous prisoner of the 1900s. He spent much of his time in this cell.

Important Features

Robben Island lies about 5.6 miles (9 kilometers) off the coast of South Africa, so it was very difficult to escape from. Anti-apartheid leader Nelson Mandela spent 18 years there. After his release, the South African government began to destroy apartheid, and he became president. The prison buildings where he was kept remain in the condition they were in when the site became a protected area. They include collapsed walls, damaged ceilings, and rusting metalwork.

Did You Know?

In 1658, a man named Autshumato became the first prisoner on Robben Island, after protesting over European settlers taking cattle belonging to his people.

Issues

The unrepaired buildings give the site a sense of hopelessness, reminding people how hard it was to fight apartheid. However, some buildings are getting worse and they need to be repaired to stop them from collapsing.

GLOSSARY

apartheid   a system run by the South African government that separated white people from non-white people

Statue of Liberty

The Statue of Liberty is located on an island in New York Harbor. The statue welcomed millions of **immigrants** arriving by boat. It is a symbol of freedom for the many different peoples who form the population of the United States.

FACT FILE

UNITED STATES

The Statue of Liberty protects the memory of many immigrants who arrived in the United States.

Category:

Criteria:

Between 1892 and 1924, 25 million immigrants were welcomed by the statue as they arrived in the United States through New York Harbor.

Statue of Liberty

pedestal

Liberty Island

TIMELINE

1886	1924	1984	1986
The Statue of Liberty is officially opened.	The statue is named a national monument.	The site is inscribed on the World Heritage List.	Restoration work is carried out for the statue's 100th anniversary.

Important Features

The Statue of Liberty is 150 feet (46 meters) high and it sits on a **pedestal** 121 feet (37 meters) high. The statue was presented to the people of the United States by the people of France to mark the 100th anniversary of the signing of the **Declaration of Independence**. The statue was created by the French sculptor Frédéric-Auguste Bartholdi.

Issues

In 1916, changes were made to the torch to make it shine more brightly, but these allowed rainwater to leak into it. The damage over the years meant that the torch had to be replaced in 1986. However, the original torch is still visible in the museum within the statue's pedestal.

The new Statue of Liberty flame is covered in gold plating.

Did You Know?
The metal framework inside the statue was created by Gustave Eiffel, who built the Eiffel Tower in Paris, France.

GLOSSARY

immigrants	people who leave one country to live in another country
pedestal	support platform
Declaration of Independence	the document declaring independence for the peoples of the United States from Great Britain

Tongariro National Park

Tongariro National Park is a mountainous, volcanic landscape on New Zealand's North Island. The highly active volcanoes of Tongariro are a symbol of the Maori's spiritual relationship with the land and their **ancestors**.

FACT FILE

North Island

NEW ZEALAND

Tongariro National Park protects three volcanoes that are **sacred** to Maori traditions.

Category:

Criteria:

The volcanic mountains of the park are Mount Tongariro, Mount Ngauruhoe and Mount Ruapehu.

Mount Ngauruhoe

Mount Tongariro

TIMELINE

260,000 years ago	A.D. 600–1300	1887	1894	1990
Volcanoes develop in the Tongariro area.	The Maori arrive in the area.	The Maori leader presents the Tongariro landscape to the people of New Zealand.	The Tongariro area becomes New Zealand's first national park.	The site is inscribed on the World Heritage List.

Important Features

The Maori believe that they are from the same family as the mountains – that they are both children of the Earth mother, Papa-tu-a-nuku, and the sky father, Rangi. They believe that the volcanoes were formed by the fire gods, Pupu and Te Hoata.

Experts believe they may never be able to clear all of the heather from Tongariro National Park.

Issues

Introduced species are changing the natural environment of the park. Heather has replaced the native red tussock shrubs on the western side. The heather cannot be sprayed with poison because that will destroy native plants. It cannot be removed by hand because that releases more seeds. Park managers are using the heather beetle from Scotland to eat the heather plants, destroying them. Tests show that the beetle only destroys the heather, while not damaging native plants.

Did You Know?
In 1995, Mount Ruapehu erupted, sending rocks 4,921 feet (1,500 meters) into the air and steam and ash up to 7 miles (12 kilometers) high.

GLOSSARY

ancestors	people who came before you in your family
sacred	holy, religious
introduced species	plants or animals that are not native to an area

Uluṟu-Kata Tjuṯa National Park

Uluṟu-Kata Tjuṯa National Park is an ancient red sandy landscape in Central Australia. The park is dominated by the massive Uluṟu rock and the Kata Tjuṯa domes. The **Indigenous Australian people** of the area call themselves Anangu. Anangu believe the landscape and its features were created by **ancestral** beings.

FACT FILE

AUSTRALIA

Uluṟu-Kata Tjuṯa National Park protects the living traditions of Anangu.

Category:

Criteria:

Kata Tjuṯa

Uluṟu

surrounding road

Uluṟu rises 1,142 feet (348 meters) above the surrounding landscape.

TIMELINE

More than 300 million years ago
Uluṟu and Kata Tjuṯa begin to form.

30,000 years ago
Humans begin living in central Australia.

1977
The area is declared a national park.

1985
Anangu are formally recognized as the traditional owners of the park.

1987
The site is inscribed on the World Heritage List.

1994
The cultural significance of the site is added to the World Heritage listing.

Important Features

The entire sandy plain, with its great rocks, is of enormous importance to Anangu. They received the knowledge of how to live from their ancestors. That knowledge is **preserved** in the landscape and in the rocks of Uluru and Kata Tjuta. The Anangu pass this knowledge to their children through art, dance, and **oral history**.

Issues

Visitors to Uluru are able to walk from the base to the top of the Uluru rock using a safety chain. This trail is sacred to Anangu and they prefer that visitors would not walk on the rock.

Anangu hope that through education people will choose not to climb the rock.

GLOSSARY

Indigenous Australian people	the first people to live in Australia
ancestral	to do with the people who came before you in your family
preserved	protected, kept safe
oral history	story of the past told in spoken words or song

Index